What is Artificial Intelligence and ChatGPT

What is Artificial Intelligence And CHATGPT?

Artificial Intelligence (AI) is the simulation of human intelligence processes by computer systems. These processes include learning, reasoning, and self-correction. The concept of AI can be traced back to the 1950s, when computer scientists first began experimenting with the idea of creating machines that could mimic human thought. However, it wasn't until recent years that AI technology has begun to reach its full potential due to advancements in computing power and the availability of large amounts of data.

AI systems can be broadly classified into two main categories: rule-based systems and machine learning systems. Rule-based systems follow a set of pre-defined rules to make decisions, while machine learning systems use algorithms to learn from data and improve over time. Machine learning is a subfield of AI that enables systems to improve their performance without being explicitly programmed.

The applications of AI are diverse and varied, and it has the potential to revolutionize many industries. Some examples of AI applications include:

Natural Language Processing (NLP): AI-powered systems can be trained to understand and respond to human language, which enables them to carry out tasks such as language translation, text summarization, and speech recognition.

Robotics: AI can be used to control and automate robots, making them more versatile and efficient in performing tasks such as manufacturing, logistics, and agriculture.

Computer Vision: AI-powered systems can be trained to understand and interpret visual data, which enables them to carry out tasks such as image recognition, object detection, and facial recognition.

Healthcare: AI can be used to assist doctors in diagnosing diseases, analyzing medical images, and developing new drugs.

Finance: AI can be used for tasks such as fraud detection, market analysis, and risk management.

Autonomous vehicles: AI is being used to develop self-driving cars that can navigate roads and make decisions without human input.

Gaming: AI is being used to create more realistic and challenging opponents in video games.

Virtual assistants: AI-powered virtual assistants, such as Amazon's Alexa or Google Assistant, can be used to control home appliances, play music, and answer questions.

It's important to note that while AI has the potential to bring many benefits, it also raises ethical and societal concerns, such as job displacement and privacy issues. It's crucial to ensure that the development and deployment of AI is done in a responsible and ethical manner, taking into consideration the potential impact on society and individuals.

AI has the potential to automate some tasks and make some jobs obsolete, but it is not likely to take over all jobs. AI is expected to change the nature of many jobs, rather than replacing them entirely. The World Economic Forum estimates that 75 million jobs may be displaced by 2022, but that 133 million new jobs may be created in their place.

The jobs that are most at risk of automation are those that involve repetitive tasks that can be easily programmed into a computer. These include jobs in manufacturing, transportation, and data entry. On the other hand, jobs that require human skills such as creativity, empathy, and critical thinking are less likely to be automated.

However, it's important to note that the displacement of jobs due to automation is not a new phenomenon. Throughout history, technological advancements have led to the displacement of jobs, but they have also led to the creation of new jobs and new industries.

It is important to consider how AI will change the nature of work and the skills that will be needed in the future. It's also important to consider how to prepare workers for the changes that are coming and to ensure that the benefits of AI are distributed fairly.

People should not be scared of AI taking over jobs, but it's important to be aware of the changes that are coming and to take steps to prepare for them. It's also important to ensure that the benefits of AI are distributed fairly and that the development and deployment of AI is done in a responsible and ethical manner.

AI, or Artificial Intelligence, refers to the simulation of human intelligence in machines that are programmed to think and learn like humans. It is a broad field of study that includes various subfields such as machine learning, natural language processing, and computer vision.

Google, on the other hand, is a multinational technology company that specializes in internet-related services and products such as search engines, online advertising, cloud computing, and software development. Google's products and services are built on top of advanced technologies, including AI.

In other words, AI is a field of study that encompasses a wide range of technologies and techniques, while Google is a company that uses these technologies to create products and services. Google uses AI in many of its products and services, such as Google Search, Google Assistant, Google Translate, and Google Photos. For example, Google uses machine learning algorithms to improve its search results, to understand and respond to voice commands in Google Assistant, to translate text between languages in Google Translate, to automatically identify and organize photos in Google Photos.

Therefore, AI is a technology that Google is using but it is not the same thing. AI is a broader concept that encompasses many fields and Google is one of the many companies that uses AI to improve its products and services.

AI is already being taught in some universities and colleges as part of computer science and engineering programs, and it is likely that the demand for AI education will continue to grow in the future. Many universities and colleges around the world have started to offer AI-related courses and even specialized degree programs in areas such as machine learning, natural language processing, and computer vision.

As for schools, it is possible that AI education may be incorporated into the curriculum in the future, but it varies from country to country and from school to school. Some schools have already started to include AI education in their curriculum, but it is still relatively rare.

As for degrees and certificates, many universities and colleges already offer degrees and certificates in AI-related fields such as computer science, data science and machine learning. Some universities have also started to offer specialized degrees and certificates in AI, such as a Master's degree in AI or a certificate in AI for business.

In conclusion, AI education is already available in universities and colleges, and it is likely that the demand for AI education will continue to grow in the future. As for schools, it varies, and there may be an increasing trend to include AI education in the curriculum. As for degrees and certificates, they are already available in AI-related fields and specialized degrees and certificates in AI are also available.

ChatGPT is a variant of the GPT (Generative Pre-training Transformer) model, which is a large language model developed by OpenAI. GPT models are pre-trained on a massive amount of text data and can be fine-tuned on specific tasks, such as language translation, question answering, and text summarization.

ChatGPT is a variant of GPT that is particularly well-suited for conversational AI applications, such as chatbots and virtual assistants. It has been trained on a large dataset of conversational text and can understand context and generate human-like responses.

GPT was first introduced in 2018 and since then, it has been improved and updated with new versions, such as GPT-2 and GPT-3. ChatGPT is one of the versions of GPT that came out after GPT-2.

You can use ChatGPT to build conversational AI applications such as chatbots, virtual assistants, and language-based games. It can be used to generate human-like responses, answer questions, and understand context in a conversation. It can also be fine-tuned on specific tasks like language translation, question answering, and text summarization. Additionally,

ChatGPT can also be used for other natural language processing tasks such as text generation, language model fine-tuning, and text-to-speech and speech-to-text.

ChatGPT is a large language model that is trained to understand and generate human-like language. It is not directly used to build robots, but it can be used to improve the language understanding and generation capabilities of robots.

Robots are typically built using a combination of mechanical engineering, electrical engineering, and computer science. They have mechanical parts such as motors, gears, and sensors that allow them to move and interact with the physical world. They also have electronic components such as microcontrollers and sensors that allow them to process information and make decisions.

The AI component of a robot often involves machine learning, computer vision, and natural language processing (NLP) to enable robots to understand, process, and respond to information from the environment. ChatGPT can be used to improve the NLP capabilities of robots and enable them to understand and generate human-like language.

ChatGPT is not used to build robots directly but it can be used to improve the language understanding and generation capabilities of robots, as part of the AI component that enable robots to understand, process, and respond to information from the environment.

In conclusion, AI is a rapidly advancing field that has the potential to revolutionize many industries and bring significant benefits to society. However, it's important to ensure that the development and deployment of AI is done in a responsible and ethical manner, taking into consideration the potential impact on society and individuals.

ChatGPT is a variant of GPT (Generative Pre-training Transformer) model, which is a large language model developed by OpenAI. GPT models are pre-trained on a massive amount of text data and can be fine-tuned on specific tasks, such as language translation, question answering, and text summarization. ChatGPT is particularly well-suited for conversational AI applications, such as chatbots and virtual assistants, and it's not used to build robots directly but it can be used to improve the language understanding and generation capabilities of robots, as part of the AI component that enables robots to understand, process, and respond to information from the environment.

It's important to note that AI has the potential to automate some tasks and make some jobs obsolete, but it is not likely to take over all jobs. AI is expected to change the nature of many jobs, rather than replacing them entirely. Therefore, it's important to be aware of the changes that are coming and to take steps to prepare for them. It's also important to ensure that the benefits of AI are distributed fairly and that the development and deployment of AI is done in a responsible and ethical manner.

www.ingramcontent.com/pod-product-compliance
Lightning Source LLC
Chambersburg PA
CBHW041154050326
40690CB00001B/467